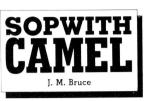

SOPWITH CAMEL

J. M. Bruce

Front cover illustration:
A 2F.1 Camel takes off from
HMS *Pegasus* in 1918; see
illustration 95.

Back cover illustrations:
Top: Camel B3751's exposed
gun installation; see illustration
9.
Below: A ditching trial being
carried out by F.1 Camel B3878
in 1918; see illustration 83.

▲ 1 ▼ 2

SOPWITH CAMEL

J. M. Bruce

ARMS AND
ARMOUR

1. The first of several Sopwith F.1 prototypes appeared just before Christmas 1916. Its upper mainplane was made in one piece and had no central cut-out; the fairing over the guns sloped upwards to the cockpit, and there was no windscreen.

2. Possibly a second prototype, this F.1 had modified fairing panels over the gun breech housings while retaining the sloping forward top decking; a small windscreen had been added. The upper wing was still a one-piece surface, but incorporated a small central cut-out that may have been made to alleviate tail-heaviness. Short ailerons, as on the first prototype, were fitted.

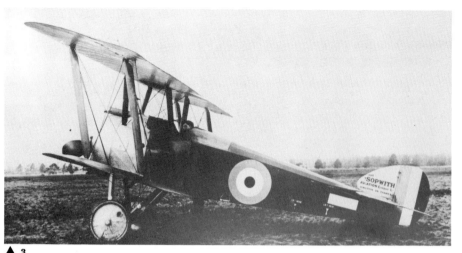

▲ 3

▲ 4　▼ 5

3. On 24 March 1917 this F.1 prototype arrived for official trials at Martlesham Heath, the locale of this photograph. Recorded by Martlesham as the F.1/3, it had the central cut-out in the upper wing, which was still a one-piece surface, and the original short-span ailerons. The top decking ahead of the cockpit was horizontal, and the aluminium cowling panels were of revised design. Although allotted the serial number B381, apparently in February 1917, this F.1 was not so reported until January 1918. It spent much time at Martlesham and Orfordness, having both standard and long-stroke Clerget engines and, by 23 May 1917, a 110hp Le Rhône. By 5 January 1918 it had been modified, apparently at Martlesham, to the so-called 'Comic' night-fighter configuration (*see* photographs 46-47). B381 was at Orfordness by 27 May 1918 and was still flying there in February 1919, latterly testing nine different types of parachute harness.

4. Apparently one of the prototypes, this F.1 was photographed at Brooklands. When photographed it had the production design of aluminium forward decking and flank panels, the latter with the large elliptical access panel that appeared on production Camels, but was still fitted with the short ailerons. More conspicuously, it had a central cut-out in the upper wing, and a Rotherham slipstream-driven petrol pump on the front starboard centre-section strut. (RAF Museum)

5. A hitherto unremarked and unnumbered F.1 prototype was delivered to the French Government. Its brief career ended late in May 1917, when it crashed while being flown by Sous-Lieutenant Canivet. It had a one-piece upper wing, the original short-span ailerons and, at the time of its demise, a 110hp Le Rhône engine, probably the first such installation in a Camel. It is perhaps significant that the position of the white rectangle

INTRODUCTION

First published in Great Britain in 1989 by Arms and Armour Press, Artillery House, Artillery Row, London SW1P 1RT.

Distributed in the USA by Sterling Publishing Co. Inc., 387 Park Avenue South, New York, NY 10016-8810.

Distributed in Australia by Capricorn Link (Australia) Pty. Ltd., P.O. Box 665, Lane Cove, New South Wales 2066, Australia.

© Arms and Armour Press Limited, 1989

All rights reserved. No part of this book may be reproduced or transmitted in any form or by any means electronic or mechanical including photocopying recording or any information storage and retrieval system without permission in writing from the Publisher.

British Library Cataloguing in Publication Data:
Bruce, J. M. (John McIntosh), 1923–
Sopwith Camel.
1. Great Britain. Royal Air Force. Sopwith fighter aeroplanes, 1914–1918
I. Title II. Series
623.74′64
ISBN 1-85409-030-5

Designed and edited by DAG Publications Ltd; printed and bound in Great Britain by The Alden Press Limited, Oxford. Line illustrations by James Goulding.

for a serial number is identical with that on the first prototype. Although there is no cut-out in the upper wing there is an indeterminate central panel, apparently secured by half-round chordwise battens between the spars. On 30 May 1917 Major-General Trenchard telegraphed a request that a replacement Camel be sent to the French; the dispatch of a production aircraft was agreed on 13 June 1917. (A. E. Ferko)

Virtually everything that has been written about the Sopwith Camel, especially by those who knew it in its time, leaves the reader in little doubt that no other aircraft of the 1914–18 war made a stronger impression on those who flew it than this stumpy, pugnacious little biplane. No pilot could be – or could afford to be – indifferent to it, least of all the pitifully young men who, often with fewer than twenty hours' flying experience, found themselves in sole and apprehensive charge of this alarmingly mettlesome aircraft.

Wilful, neurotic and savagely unforgiving to some; agile, exhilarating and enthusiastically responsive to others; the Camel came as a brusque contrast to the Sopwith Pup and Triplane, its lineal predecessors in service and combat. They were regarded with affection for their admirable flying qualities, outstanding manoeuvrability and endearingly good manners; but the inexorable demands of war soon compelled recognition that for operational purposes the standard Pup, in particular, was underpowered and under-armed. Not every Pup pilot thought that the 100hp Gnome Monosoupape was a wholly compatible replacement for its 80hp Le Rhône, and the 110hp Le Rhône was really too much for the Pup airframe; yet it was clear that more power was essential, if only to allow more weaponry to be carried.

By mid-August 1916 there was on order, by the Admiralty, a single Pup that was to have as its specified power unit a 110hp Clerget 9Z engine; it was allotted the Naval serial number N503. This was a full year before the Royal Flying Corps experimented, fruitlessly, with the 110hp Le Rhône in the Pup; but it may be that the Sopwith company recognized, even as early as the autumn of 1916, that the combination of the Clerget 9Z and the Pup airframe would not be a happy one, for no record of completion or delivery of a Pup numbered N503 has yet been found. One can only conjecture as to the possibility of a connection between design studies for N503 and the emergence, shortly before Christmas 1916, of a new Sopwith single-seat fighter, clearly derived from the Pup, but powered by a 110hp Clerget and armed with twin Vickers guns. Its Sopwith type number was F.1, but it was soon nicknamed Camel, a sobriquet inspired by the hump that housed the guns, immediately ahead of the cockpit.

Two prototypes, numbered N517 and N518, were delivered to the Royal Naval Air Service; at least one other was tested for the RFC; one went to the French Government; and a version with tapered wings, apparently known to, or distinguished by, Martlesham Heath as the F.1/1, was also evaluated. This last may have been a private venture by the Sopwith company (*but see* photograph 7).

The standard F.1 Camel was quickly ordered for both the RNAS and RFC, production being undertaken by eight contractors in addition to the parent Sopwith company. The earliest in service were with the RNAS at Dunkirk by 17 May 1917; on 25 May N6332 was transferred to the RFC to serve as an introductory sample of the type; the RFC began to receive production Camels in mid-June.

Frustrating difficulties were encountered immediately, for the first type of Kauper mechanical interrupter gear proved defective, and the gun-firing control was not on the control column; understandably, pilots did not like this arrangement. The performance of the early Clerget-powered Camels was disappointing, and urgent trials

▲ 6

6. Two F.1 prototypes, numbered N517 and N518, were delivered to the RNAS. N517 had no cut-out in the upper wing (it might, indeed, have been the first prototype), at least when it was first at Dunkirk early in March 1917. It saw operational use with Naval Squadrons Nos 9, 11 and 12, and was deleted on 21 August 1917. N518 arrived at Martlesham Heath on 13 April 1917 and spent virtually all of its career there as a trials aircraft; in this photograph, it is seen after a landing mishap. It was first tested with a 150hp A.R.1 engine in May 1917, a Humber-built B.R.1 on 15 September, various 140hp Clerget 9Bf engines from mid-October, a modified 110hp Le Rhône from early March 1918, another Clerget 9Bf in early July, and with several other modifications, fuels and lubrication systems. It survived at least until 30 November 1918.

7. An F.1 prototype with tapered wings and single, broad-chord interplane struts was tested at Martlesham Heath in May 1917; in the official Trials Report (M.101) it was recorded (with what authority is uncertain) as the Sopwith F.1/1. Its upper mainplane was made in three parts, the centre section having a rectangular cut-out between the spars; its gun and engine installations and fairings resembled those of production Camels; the undercarriage struts were of broad chord. In performance and handling characteristics the taper-wing Camel was no improvement on the standard F.1 and was taken no further. It may not have been included among the four prototypes covered by Contract No A.S.233, for as late as 12 December 1917 Contract No A.S.34594 was raised under British Requisition No 286 of 5 December for 'One experimental Sopwith Taper Wing Camel 4F.1'. This may have been merely a tidying-up procedure, but it appears that no official serial number can be connected with this aircraft. The seeming type number 4F.1 is unconfirmed, and may not be authentic (indeed, F.1/4 might have been more logical); but the contract was probably retrospective, and that designation may have been likewise.

and comparative experiments were undertaken; but the 130hp Clerget 9B was never satisfactory, and on 9 December 1917 Major-General Trenchard demanded that as many RFC Camel squadrons as possible should have the 110hp Le Rhône. Many RFC Camels in the field were subsequently converted to have this preferred power unit. In general, RNAS Camel squadrons were less affected by engine problems, for they mostly had the considerable advantage of the superior Bentley B.R.1 engine.

For night-fighting Camels the Le Rhône engine was considered essential, and numbers of these nocturnal Camels had the positions of pilot and petrol tank transposed to improve the pilot's field of view. This variant was discarded by the night-fighting squadrons in France from late July 1918 onwards.

The shipboard variant of the design, the Sopwith 2F.1, was essentially a landplane form of the Sopwith FS.1 single-seat fighter seaplane, which was listed officially as the Sopwith Improved Baby and was intended to be a replacement for the earlier Sopwith Baby seaplane, itself a direct derivative of the Sopwith SS.1 Tabloid that had originated in 1913.

To facilitate stowage on board ship, the fuselage of the 2F.1 was made in two separable sections joined behind the cockpit; the rear portion contained inflatable air bags as emergency flotation gear. Because shipboard fighters were expected to attack enemy airships, the 2F.1 retained the armament of the FS.1: a Lewis gun on an Admiralty Top Plane Mounting that enabled it to be fired upwards, and a single fixed Vickers gun.

The Sopwith 2F.1 proved its worth convincingly in two significant actions. On 19 July 1918 seven 2F.1s flew off from HMS *Furious* to make the first true carrier-launched air strike in history: a spectacularly successful bombing attack on Tondern Zeppelin base. Just over three weeks later, Lieutenant S. D. Culley flew N6812 from a towed lighter to shoot down the Zeppelin L.53.

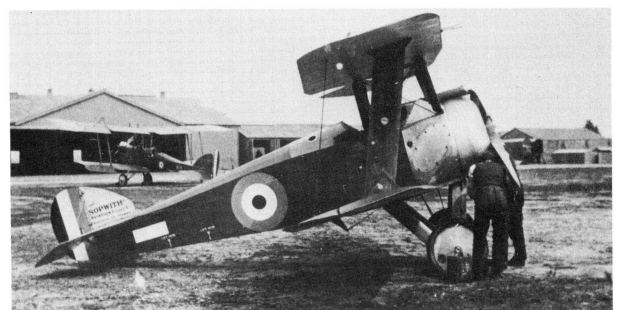

At 31 October 1918 the Royal Air Force had on charge 2,548 F.1 Camels and 129 2F.1s. Of these, 916 F.1s were with operational units in France and Italy, and 181 with Home Defence units; 112 2F.1s were with ships of the Fleet. The basic design of the aircraft had altered little in its eighteen months of operational use; it remained fully operational until the Armistice and beyond, and its production did not cease until June 1919. In the official price list of airframes and engines, the F.1 is quoted as costing £874.10s, the 2F.1 £825; the Clerget, Le Rhône and B.R.1 engines were priced, respectively, at £907.10s, £771.10s and £643.10s; instruments and guns were additional. Such were their prices: their worth could only be assessed against a more rigorous and sombre scale of values.

My warm thanks go again to those friends and fellow historians who have contributed so generously to the pictorial content of this modest compilation; as ever, to Stuart Leslie for all his help, to all those to whom photographs are attributed; and to the RAF Museum, Hendon, and the Fleet Air Arm Museum, Yeovilton, for those photographs from their collections that appear herein.

8 ▼

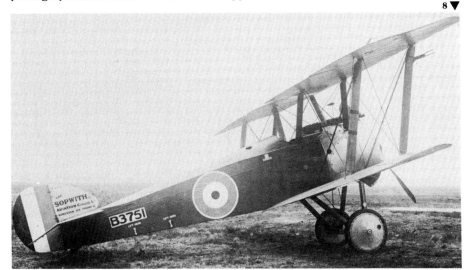

8. The first Sopwith-built production Camel for the RFC, B3751, was initially allotted to the Ascot storage depot, but on 7 June 1917 it was agreed that it should be assigned to the Technical Department for tests of gun-synchronizing gear. It went to Martlesham Heath on 15 June 1917, and by 7 July it was reported to be 'doing tests with guns and gun gear'. Reports on the first Camel that had gone to the RFC in France contained significant criticism of the gun installation: on the Camel both Vickers guns had right-hand feed, and the close fairing over them made it all but impossible to rectify stoppages of the starboard gun in combat.

9. This is probably why B3751's tested armament included this wholly exposed gun installation. By 5 January 1918 this Camel was being tested with a 150hp B.R.1 engine; by 12 January it had returned to the Sopwith works to be fitted with armour. (T. Heffernan)

10. The standard cockpit opening of the F.1 Camel, as produced in the factory, was symmetrical and enclosed the breech mechanisms of both guns. The difficulty of dealing with problems of the starboard gun was reported as early as 4 March 1917. This photograph (at Martlesham Heath) shows the various apertures in the top decking; also visible are the loading handles of the guns, the spade grip on the control column, and a mounting bracket for an Aldis optical sight. (A. R. Boeree, via E. F. Cheesman)

▲ 9 ▼ 10

11. B3761 at Brooklands in pristine condition, shortly after emerging from the Sopwith factory. This was the first and perhaps only Camel positively known to have been fitted with a starboard Vickers gun having left-hand feed; this had been installed by 16 July 1917. By 18 August it had been decided to reserve left-hand-feed guns for the Sopwith Dolphin, and to adhere to the twin right-hand-feed guns on the Camel. B3761 subsequently went to RNAS Manston (*see* photograph 29), but it is not known whether it retained its left-hand-feed starboard Vickers. Like all early production Camels it had undercarriage struts made of elliptical-section steel tubing.

12. The decision to fit only right-hand-feed guns to the Camel meant that most operational aircraft, at least in France, had the decking cut away over the starboard Vickers. At No 2 A.D. B2301 was modified in this way and tested on 19 June 1917; presumably this was the modification that was standardized for the RFC on 28 July 1917. The captured Camel seen in this German photograph had the breech housings of both guns exposed, and the shoulder of the decking was cut forward beside the starboard gun. An Aldis Sight bracket is mounted on the gun-supporting bridge member; the sight itself had probably been appropriated by a German pilot for his own use.

11 ▲   12 ▼

▲ 13

▲ 14   ▼ 15

13. The earliest deliveries of production F.1 Camels were made to the RNAS from Sopwith output of the batch N6330–N6379. One such was N6333, delivered in May 1917. At one time it was at Manston, and by 12 August 1917 it was on the strength of RNAS Eastchurch: on that date, and again on 22 August, Lieutenant A. A. Wallis flew it against raiding forces of German Gotha bombers. While at Eastchurch N6333 suffered structural failure and crashed, killing Squadron Commander A. F. Bettington. (RAF Museum)

14. Bearing the name of the popular wartime musical *Chu Chin Chow*, N6345 saw much operational service; it had a B.R.1 engine. By 7 June 1917 it was with No. 4 (Naval) Squadron, in which it was a 'B' Flight aircraft at least until August. In January 1918 it was with the Seaplane Defence Squadron, No 1 Wing, which on 15 January became No 13 (Naval) Squadron. While with No 13 Squadron N6345 was in 'A' Flight. This Camel was deleted because of general fatigue on 8 April 1918. (RAF Museum)

15. Nine of the B.R.1-powered Camels of No 201 Squadron, Royal Air Force, probably in November 1918. The three aircraft at right have white fins, 'S' having a checkerboard pattern of white squares on tailplane and elevators; on the fourth, fifth and sixth aircraft the squadron marking is closer

to the tailplane. Camel 'S', F6022, was an A.D. reconstruction of D1813 completed on 25 July 1918; D1813 had been issued to No 208 Squadron from No 1 Reception Park, Marquise, on 11 April 1918, and was also used by No 206 Squadron.

16. The B.R.1 Camels of No 3 (Naval) Squadron on the Middle Aerodrome, Dunkirk, February 1918. Personal markings can be seen on the nearest seven aircraft. B6401 has a coloured engine cowling and matching wheel covers, a playing-card painted on each lower wing, a white (?) diamond on the rear decking beside a broad white vertical bar, a chordwise white bar on the tailplane and light-coloured elevators, and a sun-ray marking on the fin. It was in 'B' Flight of No 3 (Naval), January–February 1918, saw some service at RNAS Walmer, and was written off (general fatigue) in No 213 Squadron, RAF, on 30 September 1918.

17. Of the Sopwith-built batch B3751–B3950, a total of 104 Camels (56 with Clerget, 48 with B.R.1 engines) were transferred to the RNAS. One of the Clerget Camels was B3878, a presentation aircraft, *Basutoland No 8, Makaola*. On 3 January 1918 it was with No 8 (Naval) Squadron, whose white-disc marking it bears in this photograph, together with its individual letter 'Z'. It was at the Dunkirk depot on 7 February 1918, and later went to Grain (*see* photograph No 83). (RAF Museum)

▲ 18

18, 19. On 8 March 1918, this Bentley Camel B7230 (B.R.1 engine No 337) was on the strength of No 3 (Naval) Squadron. Two days later it was brought down intact by Vfw E.

Scholz of *Jasta* 11 and its pilot, Flight Sub-Lieutenant K. D. Campbell, was made a prisoner of war. When captured, B7230 was wearing the white-disc marking of No 8 (Naval)

Squadron; presumably it had previously served with that unit. Its elevators were painted white, its engine cowling in a colour that photographed as a dark tone.

▼ 19

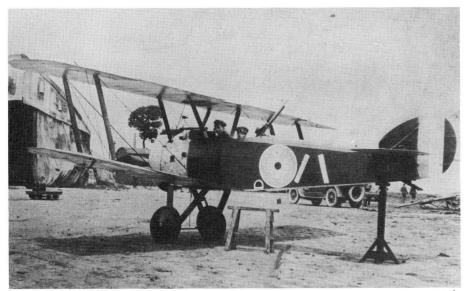

20. Camel with zumbooruk. This two-seat conversion was created by No 208 Squadron, RAF, at Serny, April – July 1918, in the hope that, to quote the late Major Christopher Draper, DSO, 'it might give the Jerry a bit of a shock'. Providing the cockpit for the rear gunner necessitated structural alterations and a smaller fuel tank placed under the pilot's seat. As the standard Camel was tail-heavy such modifications can only have aggravated this condition, yet Draper claimed that the aircraft was flown successfully. The squadron was apparently instructed to reconvert it to standard before it could be tried operationally.

20 ▲

21. Bentley Camels of No 9 (Naval) Squadron at the Middle Aerodrome, Bray-Dunes, at a time when several of the squadron's aircraft bore colourful individual markings and most carried no roundels on the fuselage. So extensive are the decorations on the nearest Camel that its serial number has been overpainted. The second is B5749, which also served with No 10 (Naval) Squadron and No 201 Squadron, RAF; it was wrecked in the latter unit on 18 August 1918. Farthest is B7155, which was at No 1 A.D. on 15 May 1918.

21 ▲   **22** ▼

22. After No 9 (Naval) Squadron was assimilated into the RAF as No 209 Squadron, its markings became the white vertical bars seen here on the fuselage of H6997. This Camel was an A.D. reconstruction to which the serial number F6326 had first been allotted in error, and was completed by 10 August 1918 (but there was also a genuine production Camel F6326 built by Boulton Paul under Contract No 35a/1302/C.1293 and delivered in early September 1918). With No 209 Squadron H6997 was flown by Lieutenant-Colonel Sidney ('Crasher') Smith, DSO, who commanded the 91st Wing; it bore the name *Dimps* on the port side by the cockpit. (RAF Museum)

▲ 23 ▼ 24

23. The cockpit of the Camel was so small that the rear ends of the Vickers guns were alarmingly close to the pilot's face. Not surprisingly, some pilots had padding fitted to the guns, seen on this aircraft, thought to be of No 209 Squadron, RAF. The forward decking has been extensively cut away over the starboard gun (and probably over the port also), a windscreen of local creation is mounted well forward, and the centre section has the enlarged cut-out. (RAF Museum)

24. The RFC standardized an Auster windscreen for use with the cut-away forward decking, but the RNAS seemingly allowed more individuality where Camel windscreens were concerned. This Camel, probably of a naval or ex-naval squadron, had an unusually comprehensive windscreen of individual or squadron design, mounted well forward. The two square-section outlets in the shoulder and flank of the fuselage were for discarded Prideaux links and empty cartridge cases; the circular tube was the carburettor air intake. (RAF Museum)

25. At one period the Camels of No 10 (Naval) Squadron must have been the most colourfully marked of any British fighter unit, with prominent horizontal stripes on the engine cowling and forward fuselage. These were a combination of white and Flight colours: 'A' Flight black, 'B' Flight red, and 'C' Flight blue. Additionally, each Camel had an individual marking on its wheel covers. B6289, a Clerget Camel, was with No 10 (Naval) in late December 1917, and by 7 February 1918 was with 'B' Flight of No 9 (Naval).

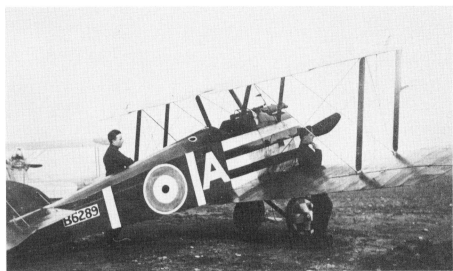

25 ▲

26. B7234 was a Bentley Camel built by Clayton & Shuttleworth, and was probably delivered in mid-January 1918. In March it was with No 13 (Naval) Squadron: N6349, seen beyond, was with that squadron by 7 February 1918. When this photograph was taken their unit had been redesignated No 213 Squadron, RAF. By July 1918 B7234 was with No 204 Squadron, was subsequently reported missing, and was deleted on 15 August. As seen here, it had a large, wide windscreen, and a single bomb-carrier, possibly for a 112lb bomb, under the fuselage.

26 ▲   27 ▼

27. Among the aircraft of No 227 Squadron at Taranto were these F.1 Camels, which joined the unit in the summer of 1918. Unfortunately their range was too limited to allow them to escort the squadron's D.H.4s to the more distant targets. The nearest Camel is C133, marked with a white vertical band behind the roundel and meeting a central white stripe along the rear decking of the fuselage; the fin is also white.

▲ 28

▲ 29　▼ 30

28. In the Aegean area, the RNAS flew Camels from Gliki, Stavros, Thermi and Mudros. In this photograph are seen three of 'F' Squadron's F.1 Camels at Mudros. At right is B3771, and the central aircraft is N6367, both Sopwith-built. N6367 also saw service with 'D' Squadron at Stavros in November 1917; on 5 May 1918 it was flown from Imbros to Mudros for exchange. (RAF Museum)

29. F.1 Camels of the War Flight at RNAS Manston, probably in 1917. Identifiable are B3843 (150hp B.R.1) and B3761 (130hp Clerget), both of which were at Manston in early July 1917 and were still on that station's strength in January 1918. At that later date they were recorded as aircraft of the RNAS War School. For an earlier note on B3761 *see* photograph No 11. (Brian Johnson)

30. A later Camel of Manston's strength was the Boulton & Paul-built F1520, which was delivered in late July 1918. The broad white band and individual letter markings appeared on several Manston-based Camels at that time, but F1520 had coloured (possibly red) stripes on the engine cowling and flank panels; its wheel covers were also coloured, with white circumferential lines. (Via *Aeroplane Monthly*)

31. The first installation of the 100hp Gnome Monosoupape engine to be officially tested in a Camel was made in B3811 in July 1917. This aircraft arrived at Martlesham Heath on 26 July; there it underwent some weeks of test flying, including trials with an oxygen cylinder; its general performance was considered to be very poor. B3811 went to the Armament Experimental Station, Orfordness, on 5 September. There it was used in experiments in fire-proofing petrol tanks; when shot at on 24 October 1917 it ignited and presumably was destroyed.

32. On 9 August 1917 B2312 arrived at Martlesham Heath, where this photograph was taken. It was the first Camel built by a sub-contractor

31 ▲

(Ruston, Proctor & Co.) to undergo official assessment; its 130hp Clerget engine was also made by Ruston, Proctor. Both engine and aircraft were adversely criticized. B2312 went to Orfordness on 30 August and had returned to Martlesham by 15 September, thereafter undertaking tests of various propellers. It was subsequently fitted with, successively, a 110hp Le Rhône, a 130hp French-made Clerget, the second B.R.1, a Badin fuel system, and a 140hp (long-stroke) Clerget, with which it was flown to the RAE, Farnborough on 6 May 1918. It was still there in February 1920, when it was fitted with Imber self-sealing fuel tanks. (RAF Museum)

33. Although installations of the 110hp Le Rhône had been made in May 1917 in two of the prototypes, scarcity of that engine delayed its use in production Camels until the autumn of 1917. Early allotments of Le Rhône Camels to the RFC in France were B6403 (9 October 1917) and B5413 (27 October); on 31 October ten Le Rhône-powered Boulton & Paul Camels were allotted. Here, with Le Rhône in place, C1581 stands in the Chelsea works of Hooper & Co., Ltd, early in 1918. On 12 February 1918 it was allotted to the RFC, France, and on 28 February went to No 80 Squadron.

32 ▲   33 ▼

▲ 34   ▼ 35   ▲ 36

34. The Le Rhône engine and other details of B5417 are visible in this German photograph taken after this Camel's capture on 9 February 1918, when Lieutenant Gerald Manley, No 54 Squadron, RFC, was taken prisoner. This Hooper-built F.1 was intended to have a 130hp Clerget, in common with most preceding aircraft of the batch B5401–B5450 and despite specification of the 110hp Le Rhône. A Le Rhône was fitted before delivery, however, and B5417 was allotted to the RFC with the Expeditionary Force on 7 November 1917. It had the later, stronger undercarriage in which the V-struts were of circular-section steel tubing with fairings added; this was introduced in September 1917. (A. E. Ferko)

35. With the 130hp Clerget 9B the Camel's performance deteriorated rapidly, and British-made Clergets were less satisfactory than French-made engines. The RFC was gravely concerned over this shortcoming, but had to accept that the six squadrons due in France by 31 December 1917 would have Clerget Camels. One of these was No 3 Squadron, RFC, whose B6385 is here seen after capture in November (Second-Lieutenant C. J. Kent, PoW); a rack for four 25lb Cooper bombs is fitted under the fuselage, and the Rotherham pump is on the forward starboard centre-section strut. (A. E. Ferko)

36. Little improvement of the pilot's upward view was offered by the standard aperture in the centre section: its primary purpose is more likely to have been the relief of tail-heaviness. Throughout January 1918 Martlesham conducted extensive tests of B6422 (110hp Le Rhône) with an enlarged cut-out, 30½ inches wide. A modified centre section with this aperture was sent to France for testing on 18 May 1918, was fitted to a Camel in 5 Brigade, and was emphatically approved. The A.S.Ds were instructed on 5 June 1918 to start modifying

37 ▲ 38 ▼

Camels in France, and the relevant formal modification F.1./78.II of 3 July was incorporated in production Camels from the autumn of 1918. Here Lieutenant S. L. Bennett of No. 3 Squadron, RAF, stands by the Le Rhône engine of his Camel, which has the enlarged cut-out, at Warloy-Baillon in the summer of 1918.

37. B6313 became a veteran and victor of many combats in the hands of Captain W. G. Barker, here at left with Lieutenants Hudson and J. Mitchell. This Camel was with No 28 Squadron while forming at Yatesbury in September 1917 and went to France with the unit on 8 October. Barker first flew it on 16 October, went to Italy with it when the squadron moved there on 12 November,

took it with him to No 66 Squadron on 10 April 1918 and to No 139 Squadron on 15 July. He flew it for the last time on 29 September 1918, having won a total of 41 confirmed victories on it. In this photograph B6313 has its identifying numeral '1' and No 28 Squadron's white-square marking repeated on the upper wing, and flight-commander's streamers on the interplane struts.

38. Built by Sopwith, B6362 was completed in late September 1917. Here, as aircraft 1 of No 28 Squadron, RFC, it is seen surrounded by French personnel, possibly while visiting a French airfield during the few weeks that No 28 Squadron spent on the Western Front before going to Italy. Its squadron marking (a white

square) was at this time repeated on the upper starboard wing, its individual numeral correspondingly on the port. Flight Commander's streamers are attached to the rear interplane struts; the engine cowling and flank panels have been painted in a dark colour that has worn badly. (Via L. A. Rogers)

39. Another of No 28
Squadron's Camels at a later
date, in Italy and probably after
the Armistice; beside it stands
its pilot, Captain Roy H. Foss, of
Sherbrooke, Quebec. Built by
Ruston, Proctor & Co., Ltd, it is
probably E1502, which had been
delivered early in July 1918.
Captain Foss made at least 90
flights in E1502. (Via K. M.
Molson)

40. On 29 August 1918 C82l5,
of No 43 Squadron, fell into
enemy hands, and Captain L. G.
Loudoun was made a prisoner of
war. This German photograph
shows how the squadron
marking was applied to the
centre section (which has the
enlarged central aperture), and
the aircraft's identifying letter 'I'
is repeated on the port upper
wing. The small lettering on the
fuselage side abaft the cockpit is
the reminder 'M T your
pockets'. This Camel had been
allotted to No 43 Squadron,
RFC, from No 1 Issues Section
on 17 March 1918. (Via L. A.
Rogers)

41. B2453, 'W' of No 46
Squadron, RFC, at Izel-le-
Hameau. Built with a Clerget
engine, this Camel was first
allotted to the Expeditionary
Force on 8 October 1917 while
still in the Ruston, Proctor
works. It was one of several
Clerget Camels that were later
fitted with Le Rhône engines,
for which transplant it was due
to go to a Repair Park in
February 1918. In this
photograph the aircraft's
identifying letter 'W' can be
seen near the inboard end of the
starboard upper mainplane; that
on the fuselage side is mostly
obscured by the officer at right.
(Trevor Foreman)

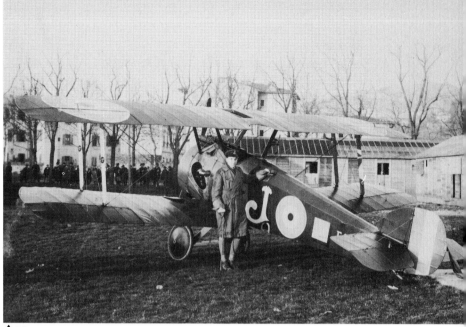

▲ 39

▲ 40   ▼ 41

42. Although the F.1 Camel saw much combat on almost every front, only one Camel pilot, Lieutenant Alan Jerrard of No 66 Squadron, was awarded the Victoria Cross. On 30 March 1918, in a sustained combat with a superior force of Austro-Hungarian Albatros D.IIIs of *Flik* 51J, he fought with outstanding gallantry, but was eventually shot down by *Oberleutnant* Benno Fiala, *Ritter* von Fernbrugg, and made prisoner of war. This photograph shows Jerrard's wrecked but heroic Camel, B5648, after coming down near Ponte di Piave. Built by Ruston, Proctor, it had been completed by 4 December 1917, on which date it was at Lincoln Aircraft Acceptance Park. (Bernd Totschinger, via L. A. Rogers)

42 ▲

43 ▲   44 ▼

43. The style, exemplary clarity and positioning, on both fuselage and rudder, of the serial number of this Hooper-built Camel are typical of the finish of the later Camels and Dolphins made by that contractor. F2168 was completed late in July 1918; as a presentation aircraft it bore the inscription 'Command Depot Alnwick' on the fuselage side at the cockpit.

44. Although of poor quality, this photograph is of unusual interest, for it depicts a standard F.1 Camel of No 44 (Home Defence) Squadron with an overwing Lewis gun supplementing the twin Vickers guns. The Lewis appears to be mounted almost directly above the attachment points of the centre-section struts, and what may have been a Bowden cable runs diagonally rearwards to the middle of the trailing-edge cut-out in the centre section. It is believed that two of No 44 Squadron's Camels had a supplementary Lewis gun.

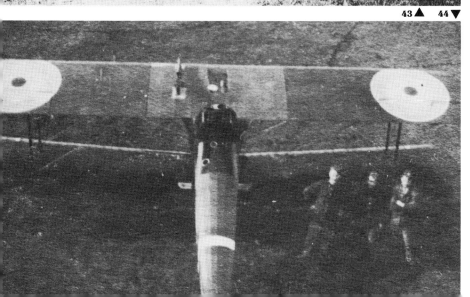

▲ 45

45. In the cockpit of D6423 sits Major C. J. Q. Brand, the officer commanding No 112 (H.D.) Squadron, who shot down a Gotha while flying this aircraft shortly before midnight on 19/20 May 1918. His Camel was a presentation aircraft, *Makhabane II*, and was probably delivered in the second week of March 1918. It was later used by No 151 Squadron. Although the white areas have been carefully obliterated from the Camel's national markings, there is a white rectangle, as if for a serial number, on the rear fuselage. (E. F. Cheesman)

46. As noted against photograph 3, the modifications that created the special night-fighting variant of the Camel (irreverently nicknamed yet officially recorded as 'Comic') were first made to B381, the F.1/3 prototype. In this photograph are seen the 'Comics' of 'C' Flight, No 44 (H.D.) Squadron, at Hainault Farm in 1918. The two nearest aircraft have small conical spinners on their propellers. (The late H. H. Russell)

▲ 46   ▼ 47

47. In the 'Comic' conversion of the Camel the cockpit was moved aft and the Vickers guns replaced by two Foster-mounted overwing Lewis guns. These could be disposed as seen in this photograph, with one at a 45° upward angle, or with both guns horizontal and parallel. This Portholme-built Camel, E5165, had stencilled serial numbers and, with E5164, was sent to No 151 Squadron in September 1918, both painted with what was enigmatically recorded as 'Special Camouflage'. On 20 July 1918 RAF Headquarters had decreed that this conversion was to be discontinued, at least as far as night-fighting Camels based in France were concerned. (Colin Owers)

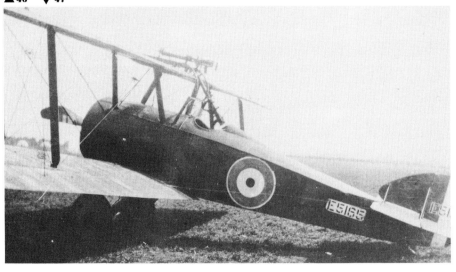

48. B9204 was built by Boulton & Paul, and the serial number on its fuselage was applied by stencil. This Camel was probably delivered in December 1917 and was used for instructional purposes. Here it is seen having its sights and port gun harmonized, the starboard gun having been removed. (RAF Museum)

49. Most Camels had the Rotherham wind-driven pump on the starboard rear centre-section strut, but it was also to be found on the starboard forward undercarriage strut or on the forward centre-section strut. At one time a majority of pilots preferred the position shown here, where the pump was visible and within easy reach for re-starting if it froze up or jammed, but it was found that the pump's vibration could split the strut and affect the sighting of the guns. On 4 August 1918 it was ruled that the pump was to be fitted to the forward undercarriage strut, which had been the standard position adopted previously by Nos 203 and 208 Squadrons. This photograph is of B9204 which, as already noted, was without its starboard gun when photographed. (RAF Museum)

50. A later Boulton & Paul Camel, H2724, also had stencilled fuselage characters but full white background for the rudder serial. This aircraft was used at No 3 Fighting School, Sedgeford, and was photographed after a mid-air collision with another Camel. H2724 sustained superficial damage to its upper starboard aileron, but the other Camel was wrecked and its pilot, Captain King, MC, killed.

48 ▲

49 ▲   50 ▼

SOPWITH CAMEL BASIC SPECIFICATION

Country of origin: Great Britain

Role: F.1 single-seat fighter; 2F.1 single-seat shipboard fighter

Power: 130hp Clerget 9B; 140hp Clerget 9Bf; 110hp Le Rhône 9J; 100hp Gnome Monosoupape 9B-2; 150hp Gnome Monosoupape 9N; 150hp A.R.1/Bentley B.R.1; experimental installations of 110hp Clerget 9Z (in first prototype), 170hp Le Rhône 9R, 185hp Clerget 9H. All were 9-cylinder air-cooled rotary engines.

Dimensions F.1:
Wingspan 28ft
Length 18ft 9in (Clerget)
  18ft 8in (110hp Le Rhône)
  18ft 6in (B.R.1 and 150hp Monosoupape)
  19ft (100hp Monosoupape and 170hp Le Rhône)
Height 8ft 6in
Wing area 231sq ft

Dimensions 2F.1:
Wingspan 26ft 11in
Length 18ft 9in
Height 8ft 10in
Wing area 221sq ft

Armament:
F.1 standard: Two 0.303in Vickers machine-guns synchronized by Kauper No. 3 interrupter gear (Clerget engine), Constantinesco C.C. gear (Le Rhône); four 25lb Cooper bombs.
F.1 modified night-fighter: Two 0.303in Lewis machine-guns on twin overwing Foster mountings.
2F.1: One fixed and synchronized 0.303in Vickers machine-gun; one 0.303in Lewis machine-gun on Admiralty Top Plane Mounting; four 25lb Cooper bombs, or equivalent.

Construction:
Basic airframe was a wire-braced wooden structure, covered with fabric and, in part, with plywood. Steel tubing was used in making such components as fin, rudder, wing-tip bends, undercarriage legs.

Finish:
Operational Camels, both F.1 and 2F.1, were finished in P.C.10, a pigmented colouring, sometimes described as Dark Khaki, that was basically mud-brown. This was normally applied to all upper and side surfaces; fabric undersurfaces were clear-doped.

Flight dates:
First prototype flew December 1916; last flight of a wartime production Camel cannot now be determined precisely, but three in Canadian service were not struck off charge until 18 October 1928. After restoration to airworthiness, the 2F.1 Camel of the Canadian National Aviation Museum, N8156, was flown on 26 May 1967, and has flown on various occasions since then.

User countries:
Great Britain, Australia, Belgium, Greece, USA, White Russian Forces, Poland, Canada, Latvia, Estonia.

WEIGHTS AND PERFORMANCE

	F.1/1	**F.1/3**	
Engine	130hp Clerget 9B	130hp Clerget 9B	140hp Clerget 9Bf
Test Report No and date	M.101 May 1917	M.86B March 1917	
Weight empty (lb)	950	929	–
Weight loaded (lb)	1,482	1,453	1,452
Max. speed (mph) at 15,000ft	106	106.5	113.5
Climb to 15,000ft	21m 5s	20m 40s	15m 45s
Service ceiling (ft)	19,000	19,000	24,000
Endurance (hrs)	2¾	2½	–

Preserved examples:
F.1
B5747, Belgian number SC-11: Musée de l'Armée et d'Histoire Militaire, Brussels, Belgium.
B7280 (fuselage only): Muzeum Lotnictwa i Astronautyki, Kraków, Poland (had been with No 201 Sqn, RAF, May 1918, later No 210 Sqn, RAF; written off 15 September 1918).
F6314: Royal Air Force Museum, Hendon, London, England (exhibited in the markings of No 65 Sqn RAF).
2F.1
N6812 (modified): Imperial War Museum, London, England. In its original form, this was the 2F.1 flown by Lieutenant S. D. Culley, RAF, when he took off from a towed lighter on 10 August 1918 and shot down the Zeppelin L.53.
N8156: National Museum of Science & Technology, Ottawa, Canada (exhibited in the Canadian War Museum, Ottawa).

PRODUCTION CONTRACTORS, F.1

Serial numbers	Contract No	Number ordered	Number delivered
SOPWITH AVIATION CO. LTD., KINGSTON-UPON-THAMES			
Probably included N517–N518, B381	A.S.233	four prototypes	four (presumed)
No number known	A.S.34594	one tapering-wing Camel 4F.1	one (presumed)
N6330–N6379	A.S.7862; C.P.102581/17	50	50
B3751–B3950	A.S.6175	200	200
B6201–B6450	A.S.6175	250	250
F7144–F7146	35a/1510/ C.1514	three	none — cancelled

B2312	B3829	N518	B3835	B3811	F1336 (USAS Camel)	F6394	B3891	N5 (2F.1 prototype)	Production 2F.1
130hp Clerget 9B	110hp Le Rhône 9J	150hp Bentley B.R.1	150hp Bentley B.R.1 modified	100hp Gnome Mono-soupape	150hp Gnome Mono-soupape	170hp Le Rhône 9R	185hp Clerget 9H	130hp Clerget 9B	150hp Bentley B.R.1
M.135 Aug 1917	M.123 July 1917	M.91 May 1917	M.134 Aug 1917	M.131 Aug 1917	M.236 Oct 1918	M.250 Feb 1919	French —	M.85 Mar 1917	— Nov 1917
962	889	977	—	882	993	1,048	—	956	1,036
1,482	1,422	1,508	1,470	1,387	1,523	1,567	—	1,523	1,530
97.5	111.5	103	114.5	102.5	107	108.5	105	104	117
23m 15s	16m 50s	20m	15m 55s	23m 15s	19m 40s	17m 30s	15m to 13,123ft	23m 40s	25m
18,500	24,000	18,000	22,000	18,500	21,500	21,500	21,000	19,000	17,300
—	—	2½	2½	2¾	2¼	—	2	3	—

Serial numbers	Contract No	Number ordered	Number delivered
BOULTON & PAUL LTD., NORWICH			
B5151–B5250	A.S.7737	100	100
B9131–B9330	A.S.7737	200	200
C1601–C1700	A.S.7737	100	100
C3281–C3380	35a/224/C.410	100	100
D6401–D6700	A.S.7737	300	300
D9231–D9380 initially allotted, perhaps in error: revised to			
D9381–D9530	A.S.37028	150	150
F1301–F1550	A.S.2164	250	250
F1883–F1957	35a/587/C.680	75	75
F6301–F6500	35a/1302/ C.1293	200	200
F9496–F9695	A.S.22398/ 1/18	200	none — cancelled
H2646–H2745	35a/2046/ C.2343	100	100
BRITISH CAUDRON CO. LTD., CRICKLEWOOD AND ALLOA			
C551–C750 originally allotted under A.S.1815/17 but cancelled, reduced to 100 aircraft, and renumbered			
C6701–C6800	A.S.12815	100	100
F9446–F9495	35a/1773/ C.1898	50	none — cancelled
H3996–H4045	35a/1657/ C.1757	50	46
J651–J680	35a/3126/ C.3625	30	none — cancelled
CLAYTON & SHUTTLEWORTH LTD., LINCOLN			
B5651–B5750	A.S.7861	100	100
B7181–B7280	A.S.7861	100	100
D3326–D3425	A.S.7861	100	100
D9581–D9680	A.S.35979	100	100
E4374–E4423	A.S.7861	50	50

Serial numbers	Contract No	Number ordered	Number delivered
F3096–F3145	35a/589/C.875	50	50
F4974–F5073	35a/1153/ C.1109	100	100
HOOPER & CO. LTD., LONDON			
B5401–B5450	A.S.12814/1/17	50	50
C1551–C1600	A.S.12814/1/17	50	50
F2083–F2182	35a/597/C.484	100	100
H734–H833	35a/2062/ C.2349	100	100
H7343–H7412	35a/3125/ C.3618	70	70
MARSH, JONES & CRIBB LTD., LEEDS			
C8301–C8400	A.S.29339	100	100
F5174–F5248	35a/1155/ C.1110	75	75
J681–J730	35a/3127/ C.3626	50	10
NIEUPORT & GENERAL AIRCRAFT CO. LTD., CRICKLEWOOD			
N6030–N6079	A.S.1362	50	none — cancelled
N6530–N6579	C.P.102627/17	50	none — cancelled
C1–C200	A.S.14412/17	200	200
F3196–F3245	35a/590/C.881	50	50
F3918–F3967	35a/1154/ C.1107	50	50
F8496–F8595	35a/1774/ C.1896	100	100
PORTHOLME AERODROME LTD., HUNTINGDON			
B4601–B4650	87/A/1836	50	50

Serial numbers	Contract No	Number ordered	Number delivered
B7131–B7180	87/A/1836	50	50
D9531–D9580	A.S.37765	50	50
E5129–E5178	A.S.2166	50	50
F1958–F2007	35a/588/C.679	50	50
F8646–F8695	35a/1786/C.1912	50	50

RUSTON, PROCTOR & CO. LTD., LINCOLN

Serial numbers	Contract No	Number ordered	Number delivered
B2301–B2550	A.S.1809/17	250	250
B5551–B5650	A.S.1809/17	100	100
B7281–B7480	A.S.1809/17	200	200
C8201–C8300	A.S.1809/17	100	100
D1776–D1975	A.S.1809/17	200	200
D8101–D8250	A.S.34277	150	150
E1401–E1600	A.S.2165/18	200	200
E7137–E7336	35a/223/C.267	200	200
F2008–F2082	35a/591/C.677	75	75
F3968–F4067	35a/1152/C.1108	100	100

Total F.1 Camel production: 5,651 plus prototypes

PRODUCTION CONTRACTORS, 2F.1

Serial numbers	Contract No	Number ordered	Number delivered

SOPWITH AVIATION CO. LTD., KINGSTON-UPON-THAMES

Serial numbers	Contract No	Number ordered	Number delivered
N4–N5 ordered as Sopwith Improved Baby Seaplanes,	A.S.26088	two	two
B6151–B6200	A.S.6174: cancelled and re-ordered as		
N6600–N6649	A.S.7862	50	50

WILLIAM BEARDMORE & CO. LTD., DALMUIR, DUNBARTONSHIRE

D4211–D4360 originally ordered as Sopwith F.1, but revised and renumbered

Serial numbers	Contract No	Number ordered	Number delivered
N6750–N6799	A.S.35920	50	50
N7100–N7149	A.S.3458 (35a/383/C.373)	50	50

(N7140–N7149 sub-contracted to Arrol-Johnston Ltd.)

FAIREY AVIATION CO. LTD., HAYES, MIDDLESEX

Serial numbers	Contract No	Number ordered	Number delivered
N7200–N7299	38a/549/C.562	100	none — cancelled

PEGLER & CO. LTD., DONCASTER

Serial numbers	Contract No	Number ordered	Number delivered
N7300–N7349	A.S.24904	50	none — cancelled

ARROL-JOHNSTON LTD., DUMFRIES (from Beardmore)

Serial numbers	Contract No	Number ordered	Number delivered
N7350–N7389	A.S.24907 (35a/663/C.695)	40	25
N7650–N7679	A.S.26353	30	none — cancelled

FREDERICK SAGE & CO. LTD., PETERBOROUGH

Serial numbers	Contract No	Number ordered	Number delivered
N7850–N7979	A.S.30951	130	none — cancelled

HOOPER & CO. LTD., LONDON

Serial numbers	Contract No	Number ordered	Number delivered
N8130–N8179	A.S.37354 (38a/906/C.947)	50	at least 30

CLAYTON & SHUTTLEWORTH LTD., LINCOLN

Serial numbers	Contract No	Number ordered	Number delivered
N8180–N8204	A.S.37750 (38a/911/C.952)	25	25

Total 2F.1 Camel production: at least 230, plus two prototypes

SERVICE USE: F.1 CAMEL, RFC AND RAF

Squadron No	Bases	Markings
WESTERN FRONT AND ITALY		
3	Warloy, Vert-Galant, Valheureux, Léchelle, Inchy	October–December 1917 two white bars on fuselage side abaft roundels; December 1917–March 1918 one white bar each side of fuselage roundel; from March 1918 two white bars ahead of fuselage roundel.
28	Yatesbury, St-Omer, Droglandt; subsequently in Italy at Milan, Ghedi, Verona, Grossa, Sarcedo, Treviso, Sarcedo	White square abaft roundel on fuselage side, on some aircraft repeated above upper wing.
43	Auchel, La Gorgue, Avesnes-le-Comte, Fouquerolles, Liettres, Touquin, Fienvillers, Senlis, Bouvincourt, Bisseghem, Cognelée, Bickendorf, Eil	September 1917–March 1918 white equilateral triangle abaft fuselage roundel; from March 1918 two sloping white bars, one each side of fuselage roundel.
45	Ste-Marie-Cappel, Fienvillers, Candas; subsequently in Italy, at Padua, San Pelagio, Istrana, Grossa. Returned to France to join Independent Force; operated from Bettoncourt and Le Hameau	White dumbbell behind fuselage roundel and centrally on rear top decking.
46	Le Hameau, Liettres, Serny, Poulainville, Cappy, Athies, Busigny, Baizieux	Two white bands on fuselage side just ahead of tailplane; from March 1918 a single lengthwise white line between cockpit and tailplane at mid-depth of fuselage side.

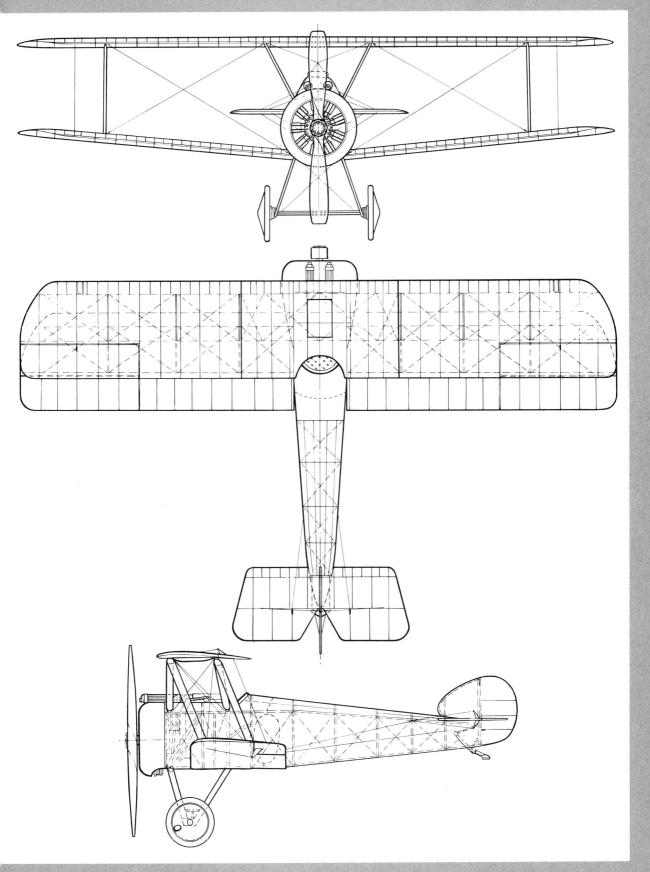

SOPWITH CAMEL

Squadron No	Bases	Markings
54	Bruay, La Houssoye, Flez, Champien, Bertangles, Conteville, Clairmarais, Caffiers, St-Omer, Vignacourt, Boisdinghem, Liettres, Touquin, Fienvillers, Avesnes-le-Comte, Rely, Merchin	White line along upper rear longeron; from March 1918 a white zigzag on fuselage sides abaft roundel.
65	La Lovie, Bailleul, Poperinghe, Droglandt, Clairmarais, Conteville, La Cappelle, Bray-Dunes, Petite-Synthe, Bisseghem	Single white horizontal bar along fuselage side, at mid-depth, from rear of cockpit to tailplane; from March 1918 two white vertical bars, one each side of fuselage roundel.
66	Estrée-Blanche, Candas; subsequently in Italy, at Milan, Verona, Grossa, Treorso, San Pietro-in-Gu, Arcade, San Pietro-in-Gu	Single white vertical bar ahead of fuselage roundel and single white horizontal bar between roundel and tailplane.
70	Liettres, Poperinghe, Marieux, Esquerdes, Droglandt, Halluin, Bickendorf	White zigzag on side of rear fuselage; from March 1918 three white vertical bands abaft roundel.
71 RFC, later 4 Sqn, AFC	Bruay, Clairmarais, Reclinghem, Serny, Auchel, Ennetières, Euskirchen, Bickendorf	White boomerang abaft fuselage roundel; from March 1918 single vertical white bar ahead of fuselage roundel.
73	St-Omer, Liettres, Champien, Cachy, Remaisnil, Beauvois, Fouquerolles, La Bellevue, Ruisseauville, Touquin, Foucaucourt, Estrées-en-Chaussée, Malencourt, Baizieux	Three vertical white bars abaft fuselage roundel; from March 1918 two such bars.
80	Boisdinghem, Serny, Champien, Cachy, Remaisnil, Wamin, Belleville Farm, La Bellevue, Fouquerolles, Liettres, Touquin, Vignacourt, Allonville, Assevillers, Bouvincourt, Bertry, Flaumont, Grand-Fayt, Strée, Clermont	Single white band round fuselage ahead of tail unit.
151	Hainault Farm, Marquise, Fontaine-sur-Maye, Famechon, Fontaine-sur-Maye, Vignacourt, Bancourt, Liettres	Single narrow white line along side of fuselage at mid-depth.
152	Carvin	None known.

MACEDONIA

17	Lahana	None known.
47	Yanesh	None known.
150	Kirech	None known.

MESOPOTAMIA

72	Baghdad	None known.

SERVICE USE: F.1 CAMEL, RNAS AND RAF

Squadron No	Bases	Markings
FRANCE		
1 Naval, from 1 April 1918 No 201, RAF	Téteghem, Ste-Marie-Cappel, Fienvillers, Noeux, Ste-Marie-Cappel, Poulainville, Noeux, Baizieux, Beugnâtre, La Targette, Béthencourt	Single vertical white bar abaft fuselage roundel.
3 Naval, from 1 April 1918 No 203, RAF	Furnes, Bray-Dunes, Walmer, Bray-Dunes, St-Eloi, Treizennes, Liettres, Filescamp, Allonville, Filescamp, Le Hameau, Bruille, Auberchicourt, Orcq, Boisdinghem	Initially colourful individual markings; from March 1918 a white circle on rear fuselage side between roundel and tailplane.
4 Naval, from 1 April 1918 No 204, RAF	Bray-Dunes, Walmer, Bray-Dunes, Téteghem, Cappelle, Téteghem, Heule	From 1 April 1918, a white equilateral triangle on fuselage side abaft roundel.
6 Naval, from 1 April 1918 No 206, RAF	Bray-Dunes	None known.
8 Naval, from 1 April 1918 No 208, RAF	Mont-St-Eloi, Walmer, Téteghem, La Gorgue, Serny, Tramecourt, Foucaucourt, Estrées-en-Chaussée, Maretz, Strée, Heumer, Eil	White disc on fuselage side abaft roundel; from March 1918 two white bars converging upwards abaft roundel.

Squadron No	Bases	Markings
9 Naval, from 1 April 1918 No 209, RAF	Le Hameau, Dunkerque, Leffrinckhoucke, Dunkerque, Dover, Dunkerque, Téteghem, Bray-Dunes, Cappelle, Bailleul, Clairmarais, Bertangles, Quelmes, Bertangles, Le Hameau, Bruille, Saultain, Froidmont	Apparently only personal markings on Camels while 9 (Naval) Sqn; from March 1918 one vertical white bar ahead of fuselage roundel and two abaft thereof.
10 Naval, from 1 April 1918 No 210, RAF	Droglandt, Leffrinckhoucke, Téteghem, Treizennes, Liettres, St-Omer, Ste-Marie-Cappel, Téteghem, Boussières-en-Cambrésis	Two vertical white stripes, one each side of fuselage roundel, at one period supplemented by multiple line-of-flight stripes on nose and forward fuselage, in white and Flight colour; from March 1918 white horizontal dumbbell abaft fuselage roundel.
13 Naval, from 1 April 1918 No 213, RAF	St-Pol, Bergues, Stahlhille	None known.
No 471 Flight, RAF	Walmer	None known

AEGEAN GROUP

Squadron No	Bases	Markings
C Squadron, RNAS; from 1 April 1918 No 220 Sqn, RAF	Gliki	
D Squadron, RNAS; from 1 April 1918 No 221 Sqn, RAF	Stavros	
F Squadron, RNAS	Thermi, Mudros	At least one F.1 Camel (B5668) and one 2F.1 photographed at Mudros had a single horizontal white bar along the fuselage side, at mid-depth, from rear of cockpit symmetrical about the roundel.
No 222 Sqn, RAF	Thasos	

ADRIATIC GROUP

Squadron No	Bases	Markings
224 Squadron, RAF	Otranto	None known on Camels.
225 Squadron, RAF	Andrano	None known on Camels.
226 Squadron, RAF	Taranto, Otranto, Lemnos, Taranto	None known on Camels.
227 Squadron, RAF	Taranto	Camel C133 had a vertical white band around the rear fuselage immediately behind the roundel; no other marking known (see photograph No 27).

HOME DEFENCE, RFC/RAF

Squadron No	Bases	Markings
37	Stow Maries, Goldhanger, Biggin Hill, Rochford	No squadron marking known.
39	Hounslow, Woodford, Biggin Hill, Hainault Farm, North Weald, Sutton's Farm	No squadron marking known.
44	Hainault Farm, North Weald, Bassett	Single vertical white band around rear fuselage abaft roundel; some Camels had three vertical bars abaft the roundel, apparently in Flight colour combinations.
50	Bekesbourne	At least one Camel bore an emblem of two leaping dingoes in white on fuselage side at the cockpit.
51	Mattishall, Tydd St Mary, Marham	None known on Camels.
61	Rochford	None known.
78	Sutton's Farm, Biggin Hill	None known.
112	Throwley	None known.
143	Detling	At least four of No. 143's Camels had about ¾ of the diameter of the wheel covers painted white, but this might have been merely a Flight marking.

Squadron No	Bases	Markings
HOME DEFENCE, RNAS SHORE STATIONS IN ENGLAND		
	Dover, Eastchurch, Isle of Grain, Manston, Walmer	None known.
US AIR SERVICE SQUADRONS, FRANCE		
17th Aero	Petite-Synthe, Auxi-le-Château, Doullens, Toul	White dumbbell on side of rear fuselage.
41st Aero	Colombey-les-Belles, Lay-St-Remy, Coblenz	Within an ellipse (upper half grey, lower yellow), a picture of a Camel with pyramids (as on a packet of Camel cigarettes) on fuselage side at rear of cockpit. More usually, a camel partly superimposed on a capital letter 'V'.
148th Aero	Cappelle, Allonville, Remaisnil, Baizieux, Le Cateau, Le Quesnoy, Toul	While operating with RAF, white equilateral triangle abaft roundel.
185th Aero (night-fighting)	Rembercourt	Silhouette of a bat (black) against a full moon (yellow).
AVIATION MILITAIRE BELGE		
1ère Escadrille (few only)	Houthem	None known on Camels.
4éme Escadrille (few only)	Hondschoote	None known on Camels.
6éme Escadrille (few only)	Houthem	None known on Camels.
9éme Escadrille (briefly)	Les Moëres	None known on Camels.
11éme Escadrille	Les Moëres	Cocotte in white on fuselage side.
RUSSIA		
47, RAF, 'B' Flight	Novorossisk, Ekaterinodar, Beketovka	At least one Camel had a horizontal white bar on the side of the nose and forward fuselage, with a further white bar at an angle of about 45° across the rudder; Russian roundels.
221, RAF	Baku, Petrovsk	None known on Camels.
RAF Contingent	Archangel	None known.
Slavo-British Aviation Group	Bakeritza	None known.
POLAND		
7th Kościuszko, 1920	Holoby, Lwów	The Kościuszko badge: vertical red and white stripes within a white circle bearing blue stars; at the centre a red cap outlined in black, on the intersection of two scythes in saltire.
USA, POST-WAR		
US Navy	Allocated to USS *Texas*, USS *Arkansas*	None known.

SERVICE USE: 2F.1 CAMEL, RNAS AND RAF

Shipboard use from HM Ships: Aircraft Carriers *Manxman*, *Pegasus*, *Argus*, *Vindictive*; battleships, cruisers and battle cruisers *Ajax*, *Aurora*, *Australia*, *Barham*, *Birkenhead*, *Caledon*, *Calliope*, *Canada*, *Carlisle*, *Caroline*, *Cassandra*, *Chatham*, *Comus*, *Cordelia*, *Courageous*, *Delhi*, *Dublin*, *Emperor of India*, *Galatea*, *Glorious*, *Inconstant*, *Indomitable*, *Inflexible*, *Iron Duke*, *Lion*, *Malaya*, *Melbourne*, *New Zealand*, *Orion*, *Penelope*, *Phaeton*, *Princess Royal*, *Queen Elizabeth*, *Ramillies*, *Renown*, *Repulse*, *Revenge*, *Royalist*, *Royal Oak*, *Royal Sovereign*, *Southampton*, *Sydney*, *Tiger*, *Undaunted*, *Valiant*, *Warspite*, *Yarmouth*.

Also flown from shore stations in Britain, e.g. Felixstowe, Great Yarmouth (No 212 Sqn, RAF), Isle of Grain, Turnhouse, Manston, East Fortune, Cranwell, Leuchars.
Aegean: Mudros. **Baltic:** Koivisto. **Canada:** Camp Borden (post-war). **Estonian Air Service:** one only (N6616). **Latvian Air Service:** probably three only, 1920.
Markings: In general, 2F.1 Camels in British service carried no unit or ship markings, but some aircraft of No 212 Squadron, RAF, Great Yarmouth, had a single vertical white bar abaft the fuselage roundel; and N6822 of HMAS *Sydney* had a shallow arrow-head in white immediately abaft the fuselage roundel.

51. Even in 1918 the characteristic stance of Winston Churchill was unmistakable. Here he is seen at the Armament Experimental Station, Orfordness, in October 1918, with Lieutenant-Colonel A. Shekleton, DSO, and Camel B2538. Yet another built by Ruston, Proctor, B2538 was at Orfordness throughout 1918, and was used in air-firing tests of guns and gun-lubricating oils. Originally powered by a 130hp Clerget engine, it had been fitted with a 110hp Le Rhône by 31 March 1918.

51 ▲

52. Believed to be of No 4 Fighting School, Freiston, this Ruston, Proctor Camel had padding on its gun butts and a windscreen that suggested earlier service with a Naval squadron. The officers are Major H. S. Kerby, DSC, and Captain E. D. G. Galley, MC. Flying a Sopwith Pup, Kerby shot down a Gotha on 12 August 1917 and had a share in the destruction of another on 22 August.

52 ▲   53 ▼

53. The 100 F.1 Camels H734–H833 built by Hooper were specifically ordered as night-fighters but, perhaps as a consequence of the RAF's decision of 20 July 1918 to abandon the 'Comic' conversion, were delivered in standard form. This is exemplified by H739, believed to be of No 44 (Home Defence) Squadron, RAF, which was delivered in mid-August 1918. Here it is seen with navigation lights, flare brackets, and night-flying markings as external evidence of its operational function. (Stewart Taylor, via K. M. Molson)

▲ 54

▲ 55　▼ 56

54. At training establishments some Camels – probably the personal aircraft of senior instructors – were given colourful markings. This one was at No 1 School of Aerial Fighting, Ayr. It was probably a Ruston, Proctor Camel, but its enthusiastically comprehensive paint scheme had obscured its serial number. The third aircraft in the line had a checkerboard area on its rear fuselage. (Alex Revell)

55. Very much a personalized Camel, this one had no national markings on any surface visible in this photograph. The fuselage, fin and wheel covers may have been blue; the rudder had multi-colour checks; the ailerons and elevators had alternate rib spaces painted white; a coloured streamer is attached to each rear interplane strut. The monogram on the fuselage is that of Lieutenant O. W. A. Manning, who is standing by the aircraft. As on many training Camels, the gun positions were faired over. (Via K. M. Molson)

56. Checkered markings were popular on instructors' Camels. This one appears to have been F6491 which, built by Boulton & Paul, was delivered about mid-October 1918. The numerals of the serial number are painted under the lower wings, each to a square, while an unusually small roundel is painted on a white square. (RAF Museum)

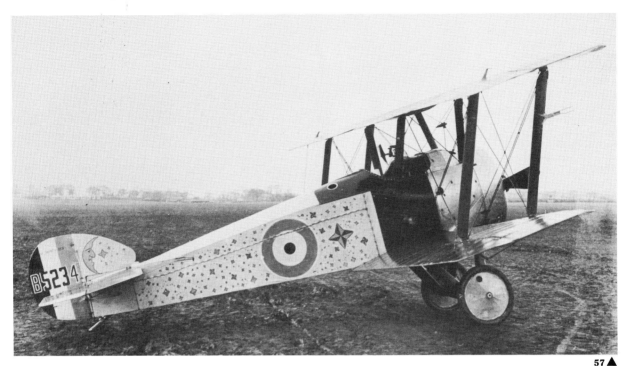

57. Also built by Boulton & Paul, but rather earlier than F6491, B5234 was completed in November 1917. In 1918 it was an aircraft of 'A' Flight of the Wireless Experimental Establishment, Biggin Hill, where it wore – possibly in post-Armistice euphoria – this whimsically astral scheme of decoration.

58. White-painted Camels were also to be seen at training units, probably favoured by senior instructors or Wing Examining Officers. The identity of this Clerget-powered specimen is not known, but the following Camels were, at one time or another, given all-white finishes: B5157 (*see photographs Nos 61 and 62*); B7369; C8, the personal aircraft of Wing Commander E. L. Conran, possibly also used at No 31 Training Depot Station, Fowlmere; C42, later converted to a two-seater and still in service at Leuchars in July 1919; and C123 (*see photographs Nos 59 and 60*). (RAF Museum)

59, 60. With the Australian Flying Corps Training Wing at Leighterton was this white Camel, C123. It bore the additional and appropriate emblem of an emu on a dark (presumably red) panel on the fuselage side, and had a coloured (presumably blue) circle on each wheel cover. Built by the British Nieuport Co., C123 had the unusual refinement of small fairings behind the carburettor breather tubes; it was flown by Captain E. F. Pflaum, who had earlier seen combat on S.E.5a's with No 2 Squadron, AFC, and subsequently on Camels with No 4 Squadron, AFC. (Via Colin Owers)

61, 62. The school of Special Flying at Gosport had coloured Camels. B5157 was a Boulton & Paul product that, as seen in the first photograph, was delivered to Gosport in standard form and finish, with guns installed; it had been completed by late September 1917. In its white paint scheme it had no guns, and the forward top decking was modified to slope down to the engine cowling, thus giving improved forward view. Surprisingly, its Rotherham pump had been removed.

63. Gosport's other coloured Camels were B6446, which was red, and B5584, which was mauve. The former was short-lived, but B5584 is seen here with Captain D. Milner-Deighton (seated), commander of 'A' Flight of the School of Special Flying, and Lieutenant F. Dudley Hobbs. B5584 was one of the 1,575 Camels built by Ruston, Proctor & Co., Ltd, and had been completed in late November 1917. This Camel had a small spinner, and its struts and wheel covers were painted in a light colour, probably white. Like the white-painted B5157 it was gunless and its forward decking had been similarly modified, but it retained its Rotherham pump.

▲ 59

▲ 60   ▼ 61

62 ▲   63 ▼

▲ 64

65 ▶

64, 65. A Camel that was used for advertising, in a good and patriotic cause, was B6416 of Shawbury (probably No 9 TDS). It was liberally inscribed with exhortations to buy War Bonds. Sopwith-built and completed early in October 1917, it was with No 73 Squadron, RFC, later that month; by February 1918 it was with No 10 Training Squadron, Gosport. Unfortunately, in a mishap at Ludlow it found itself in the undignified attitude seen in the second photograph.

66. Built by Clayton & Shuttleworth, Ltd, as one of the batch B7181–B7280, this Camel had the unusual modification of a hinged access panel in the side of the fuselage abaft the main petrol tank. The aircraft's identity cannot be established precisely, because its serial number, originally applied in black on the fin, appears to have been painted out.

▼ 66

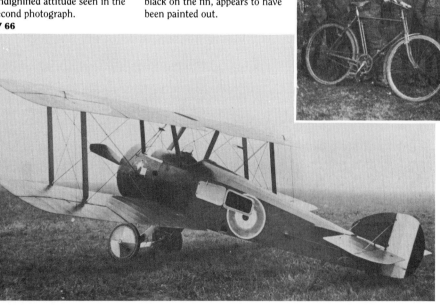

67. C6753 is here seen at Montrose, probably with No 32 TDS, with Lieutenant H. Johnson in the cockpit and Lieutenant L. V. West behind him. This Camel had earlier been used by No 151 Squadron, RAF, and was recorded at No 2 Aircraft Supply Depot, Berck-sur-Mer, on 26 June 1918. At Montrose it retained a dark-green finish probably acquired for No 151 Squadron's night-fighting duties, and it had no rudder stripes. The triple white bands and the numeral '3' were local Montrose markings.

68. Another of Montrose's Camels was F9409, an aircraft that had been assembled from salvage by No 3 (Western) Aircraft Repair Depot, Yate, and numbered in the batch of serials F9396–F9445 allotted in mid-1918 for such rebuilds. The presence of the substantial padding on the breech casings of the guns suggests that it may have become a standard feature on Camels by late 1918.

69. An F.1 Camel that lingered on in RAF service after the Armistice was F4021, seen here at Collinstown, Ireland, in 1919. Its lack of armament is plain to see, and it may have been an aircraft of No 24 TDS, which had formed at Collinstown in August 1918 and disbanded in 1919. F4021 was completed by Ruston, Proctor late in October 1918.

67 ▲

68 ▲   69 ▼

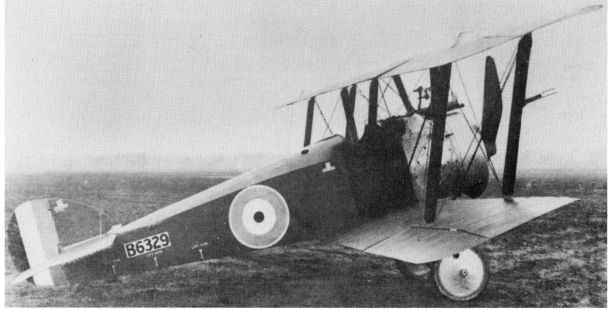

▲ 70

70. B6329 was Sopwith-built and was probably delivered in early September 1917. Fitted with a 150hp Gnome Monosoupape 9N engine, it arrived at Martlesham Heath for trials on 15 November 1917. After performance and engine tests it went to the AES, Orfordness, on 25 January 1918. Although it was supposed to return to Martlesham after 50

▼ 71

hours' more flying, it was reported to suffer from vibration, and by 13 April 1918 its Monosoupape had been replaced by a 130hp Clerget, which it apparently retained thereafter. At Orfordness B6329 flew a great deal, was used in gunnery and bombing trials, and even set off, on 31 May 1918, to look for reported German seaplanes. It was still at

Orfordness on 26 August 1918, on which date its pilot (Captain R. M. Charley) noted that it was 'not safe'.

71. Many of the 143 Camels supplied to the US Air Service in 1918 had the 150hp Monosoupape engine. This one, possibly F1336, was tested at Martlesham Heath, wearing American roundels, as seen

here. The first such Camel, D6567, had arrived at Martlesham on 4 July 1918 but crashed as a result of engine failure before 20 July. F1336 arrived on 24 July and underwent the official trials: these were delayed until early September by engine trouble, and the aircraft did not leave Martlesham until 8 November 1918.

72. Bearing American roundels but no other markings, this Camel (identity unknown) was photographed during a ground run of its engine. Unsurprisingly, it was built by Boulton & Paul, as were the very large majority of the Camels supplied to the USAS. An unusual fitting on this aircraft was the uncovered framework of a head fairing similar to that of the 'Comic' night-fighter variant.

73. A Camel in American service bearing a form of the bat emblem of the 185th Aero Squadron, USAS. Its seemingly white-painted fuselage and tail surfaces are incongruous, for the 185th was formed as a night-fighter unit. Behind the Camel are several Spads 13, to which type the 185th had been fully converted by 1 December 1918. Perhaps this Camel was retained post-Armistice as a practice or personal aircraft.

74. The first Camel to receive a Belgian number was B5710, seen here in Belgian colours, retaining its RFC serial number but with the additional marking (in the middle stripe on the rudder) of 'SK 1'. In Belgian service the prefix was later changed to SC, and at least 57 further Camels were transferred to the *Aviation militaire belge*. B5710 was transferred from RNAS strength, as were seven other Camels transferred by the end of March 1918.

72 ▲

73 ▲   74 ▼

▲ 75

▲ 76 ▼ 77

75, 76. Another exported RNAS Camel was B3891, which was allotted to the French Government. In this French photograph it is seen with a small access hatch in the fuselage side in much the same position as seen on the Camel in photograph No 66. On the rear interplane strut are leads for an absent boom-mounted static/pressure head for an air-speed indicator. This Camel had a 130hp Clerget 9B engine when this photograph was taken, but the French authorities used it as a flying test-bed for later experimental rotary engines that included the 185hp Clerget 9H and the 170hp Le Rhône 9R. The latter is seen in the second of these two photographs; the boom-mounted static/pressure head is in place.

77. The 170hp Le Rhône 9R was flown and tested at Martlesham Heath in this F.1 Camel, F6394. It arrived at Martlesham on 25 September 1918, fitted with a 140hp Clerget 9Bf but designated as test aircraft for the Le Rhône, which had been installed by 12 October. Its tests of performance, consumption and general engine running continued with undiminished priority beyond the Armistice, and it is known to have been flying until mid-February 1919. Apart from modifications necessitated by the dimensions of the Le Rhône, F6394 had an enlarged rudder (*see* next photograph).

78. The strong torque reaction that was a marked characteristic of the Camel required swift and decisive use of the rudder, and the effectiveness of the standard surface was only just adequate. An enlarged rudder was designed at Martlesham Heath and tested in the late summer of 1918; its drawing was dated 18 September 1918, and it provided 32 per cent more area than the standard surface. Advice that two of these rudders were to be sent to France was given on 7 October, and they were dispatched on 23 October; but, sent in error to No 43 Squadron, they were never used. This Ruston, Proctor Camel, photographed at the Isle of Grain, may have been E7274, which was tested there on 16 December 1918 by Lieutenant-Colonel Harry Busteed, fitted with a fin and rudder of 3.5sq ft additional area and extended tailplane and elevators with an extra 6.4sq ft. E7274 continued similar tests with an even larger fin and rudder, finally crashing on 1 February 1921.

79. Photographed at Beamsville, Ontario, in 1918, B3772 was sent to Canada, apparently via the USA, in 1917 for use as an instructional airframe at the School of Aeronautics, University of Toronto. Captain A. E. Godfrey, MC (ex No 40 Squadron, RFC; twelve victories), Officer Commanding the School of Aerial Fighting, Beamsville, 'rescued' the Camel, had it restored to airworthiness, and flew it to demonstrate to his cadets the qualities of an operational fighter. (K. M. Molson)

80. So many Camels were crashed by inexperienced pilots at training units, too often with fatal results, that a two-seat dual-control conversion was devised, probably at South Carlton at the suggestion of Lieutenant-Colonel L. A. Strange, where the structural work was undertaken by Lieutenant Morgan (but in recent times it has been claimed that the first conversion was made in 1917 at Montrose on the initiative of Major H. V. Champion de Crespigny). The main fuel tank was removed and replaced by the rear seat; a limited petrol supply was carried in a small gravity tank in front of the forward cockpit. (The late Rodney Gerrard)

78 ▲

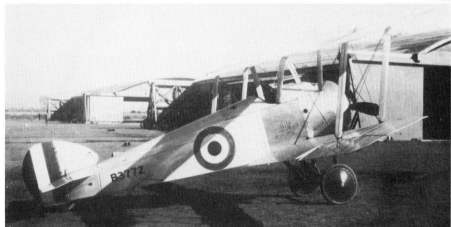

79 ▲   80 ▼

▲ 81

81. It seems that at least 24 two-seat conversions were made, one of them being B2504 of No 32 TDS, Montrose, seen here wearing fuselage markings similar to those of the standard C6753 (photograph 67). This two-seater had a Clerget engine, presumably a 9B of 130 horse power.

82. From the summer of 1918 until the end of that year, experiments in carrying Camels under rigid airships and launching them in flight were conducted; most of the aeroplanes used were 2F.1 Camels. On 20 May 1920 this Hooper-built F.1 Camel, H7363, was dropped, unmanned, from the airship R.33 with engine running, in a test of the Imber self-sealing petrol tank. In the ensuing crash the fuel tank was smashed but no fire followed. This Camel had been at the RAE, Farnborough, in February 1920, with an Imber tank installed. (K. M. Molson)

83. Throughout much of the 1914-18 war many valuable experiments in various aspects of naval flying were conducted at the Isle of Grain. These included the development of hydrovanes and inflatable air bags to enable ditched aircraft to alight in reasonable safety and float thereafter, to give their crews better hope of survival. One of the trials aircraft was the F.1 Camel B3878, formerly of No 8 (Naval) Squadron (*see* photograph 17), seen here after making the second trial ditching successfully on 9 August 1918. It had a main hydrovane on the undercarriage and a small one on the tailskid.

▲ 82 ▼ 83

84 ▲

84. For the third ditching trial an extended and strengthened hydrovane was mounted well ahead of the wheels, which were of smaller than standard diameter. This photograph is dated 3 September 1918, and a successful ditching was effected next day. The Camel B6229 was also used in the Grain ditching trials, but it cannot be confirmed that it was the subject of this photograph.

85. The flying of Camels from lighters towed by destroyers was developed in 1918 and resulted in the destruction of the Zeppelin L.53 on 11 August 1918. Experiments continued thereafter: this photograph, dated 6 November 1918, depicts a much modified F.1 Camel in position on a lighter, its tailskid on a Tail Guide Trestle. The aircraft, F3128, has a B.R.1 engine and jettisonable undercarriage; its starboard Vickers gun has been removed, but there are two Admiralty Top Plane Mountings on the centre section to accommodate two Lewis guns. Eight cables and two axle clamps secure the Camel to the lighter's deck.

86. In the immediate post-war period the US Navy had six F.1 Camels. These had the American naval numbers A5658, A5659 (both with 165hp Gnome Monosoupape engines), A5721, A5722, A5729 and A5730 (all four with Clergets). A5721 is here seen at Guantanamo in March 1920, equipped with Grain Flotation Gear and fitted with a wind-driven generator on the fuselage side. (Fred C. Dickey, Jnr)

85 ▲   86 ▼

▲ 87 ▼ 88

87. One of the US Navy's Clerget-powered F.1 Camels with port wheel jettisoned and port air bag inflated. Its hydrovane is in the final position determined by the Grain experiments. (US Navy)

88. It has been reported that at least one F.1 Camel, possibly an ex-47 Squadron aircraft, was captured by Bolshevik forces on the Southern Front in 1920; and it is believed that a few others were later flown by Russian pilots. The gunless (and possibly engineless) Camel seen in this somewhat inadequate photograph has a star painted on its rudder, while the fuselage side bears a large emblem consisting of a bat with outstretched wings, above a two-bladed propeller and with a skull and crossbones superimposed. (Robert Gretzyngier, via Colin A. Owers)

89. Two prototypes of the Sopwith FS.1, a single-seat fighter seaplane, officially designated Sopwith Improved Baby, were ordered as N4 and N5. The first of these may have been the 'Camel seaplane' that was reported wrecked in March 1917. N5 was apparently built with a wheel undercarriage, and is here seen at Brooklands soon after completion, with its Lewis gun mounted inverted on the centre section in the manner intended for the FS.1. This prototype of the 2F.1 went to Martlesham Heath on 15 March 1917 for official trials, was at the Isle of Grain by 4 April 1917, and was still in commission in March 1918. (Fleet Air Arm Museum)

89 ▲

90. Dated 7 June 1917, this photograph is of N5 at the Isle of Grain, fitted with eight launching tubes for Le Prieur rockets on the interplane struts, and a wind-driven generator, seen in the stowed passive position on the fuselage side. The latter provided power for a W/T set. Metal sheathing had been applied to the upper surface of the lower wings as protection against the rockets' efflux, and the Lewis gun was by this time carried right way up on an Admiralty Top Plane Mounting: it is here seen at or near maximum elevation.

90 ▲   91 ▼

91. Production 2F.1 in assembly at the Beardmore works. This photograph shows the steel-tubing centre-section struts and the mounting of the Lewis gun; also visible are the turnbuckles that secured the two separable portions of the fuselage together, and the external rocker for the elevator controls. N7139 was test-flown by A. Dukinfield-Jones on 11 October 1918 and delivered to Renfrew that day. It was later in HMS *Undaunted*. (Chaz Bowyer).

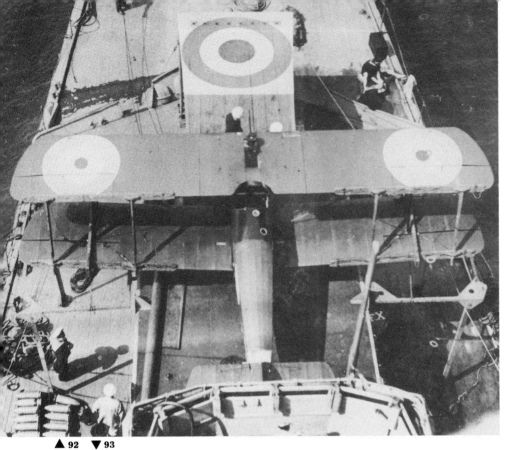

92. The practice of flying-off fighter aircraft with wheel undercarriages from minute flight platforms on cruisers had been pioneered by the Camel's predecessor, the Sopwith Pup. Here a 2F.1 Camel stands on the platform of a *Chatham*-class light cruiser: these platforms often bore a marking such as the roundel seen on this ship. The Camel has external control locks fitted. (RAF Museum)

93. On capital ships a flight platform was built on to a gun turret, which could then be turned into the 'felt' wind and an aircraft launched without the ship having to steam into true wind. N6617, a Sopwith-built 2F.1, stands on the flight platform of HMS *Renown*, its tailskid on the Tail Guide Trestle, its security devices including two wide bands of canvas over the rear fuselage. Earlier, in December 1917, N6617 had been in, or allocated to, HMS *Nairana*. (Fleet Air Arm Museum)

▲ 92   ▼ 93

94. An atmospheric impression of HMS *Glorious'* Camel running its engine on the ship's gun-turret flight platform. The aircraft has markings on its wheel covers, and it appears that the engine cowling and flank panels are of the same colour as the dark ring and centre of the wheel covers. Sopwith 2F.1s known to have been in, or allocated to, HMS *Glorious* were N6605, N7117 and N7121. (Fleet Air Arm Museum)

94 ▲

95. 2F.1 Camels were also taken aboard the carrier vessels HMSs *Manxman* and *Pegasus* in 1918, where they had the benefit of somewhat larger flying decks. This photograph captures one of a series of take-offs from HMS *Pegasus*. The Camel's identity is not known, but the ship had, probably at various times, N6603, N6611, N6788, N6820, N6826 and N6836.

95 ▲   96 ▼

96. At least eight 2F.1 Camels continued to fly operationally in 1919. They were taken to the Baltic in HMS *Vindictive* to oppose Bolshevik forces in that area, and operated from a primitive land base at Koivisto, where this photograph was taken. Here a 2F.1 is about to have its engine started; in addition to its standard installation of Vickers and Lewis guns it has small bombs in a rack under the fuselage. (RAF Museum)

The *Fotofax* series

A new range of pictorial studies of military subjects for the modeller, historian and enthusiast. Each title features a carefully-selected set of photographs plus a data section of facts and figures on the topic covered. With line drawings and detailed captioning, every volume represents a succinct and valuable study of the subject. New and forthcoming titles:

Warbirds
F-111 Aardvark
P-47 Thunderbolt
B-52 Stratofortress
Stuka!
Jaguar
US Strategic Air Power:
 Europe 1942–1945
Dornier Bombers
RAF in Germany

Vintage Aircraft
German Naval Air Service
Sopwith Camel
Fleet Air Arm, 1920–1939
German Bombers of WWI

Soldiers
World War One: 1914
World War One: 1915
World War One: 1916
Union Forces of the American
 Civil War
Confederate Forces of the
 American Civil War
Luftwaffe Uniforms
British Battledress 1945–1967
 (2 vols)

Warships
Japanese Battleships, 1897–
 1945
Escort Carriers of World War
 Two
German Battleships, 1897–
 1945
Soviet Navy at War, 1941–1945
US Navy in World War Two,
 1943–1944
US Navy, 1946–1980 (2 vols)
British Submarines of World
 War One

Military Vehicles
The Chieftain Tank
Soviet Mechanized Firepower
 Today
British Armoured Cars since
 1945
NATO Armoured Fighting
 Vehicles
The Road to Berlin
NATO Support Vehicles

The *Illustrated* series

The internationally successful range of photo albums devoted to current, recent and historic topics, compiled by leading authors and representing the best means of obtaining your own photo archive.

Warbirds
US Spyplanes
USAF Today
Strategic Bombers, 1945–1985
Air War over Germany
Mirage
US Naval and Marine Aircraft
 Today
USAAF in World War Two
B-17 Flying Fortress
Tornado
Junkers Bombers of World War
 Two
Argentine Air Forces in the
 Falklands Conflict
F-4 Phantom Vol II
Army Gunships in Vietnam
Soviet Air Power Today
F-105 Thunderchief
Fifty Classic Warbirds
Canberra and B-57
German Jets of World War Two

Vintage Warbirds
The Royal Flying Corps in
 World War One
German Army Air Service in
 World War One
RAF between the Wars
The Bristol Fighter
Fokker Fighters of World War
 One
Air War over Britain, 1914–
 1918
Nieuport Aircraft of World War
 One

Tanks
Israeli Tanks and Combat
 Vehicles
Operation Barbarossa
Afrika Korps
Self-Propelled Howitzers
British Army Combat Vehicles
 1945 to the Present
The Churchill Tank
US Mechanized Firepower
 Today
Hitler's Panzers
Panzer Armee Afrika
US Marine Tanks in World War
 Two

Warships
The Royal Navy in 1980s
The US Navy Today
NATO Navies of the 1980s
British Destroyers in World
 War Two
Nuclear Powered Submarines
Soviet Navy Today
British Destroyers in World
 War One
The World's Aircraft Carriers,
 1914–1945
The Russian Convoys, 1941–
 1945
The US Navy in World War
 Two
British Submarines in World
 War Two
British Cruisers in World War
 One
U-Boats of World War Two
Malta Convoys, 1940–1943

Uniforms
US Special Forces of World
 War Two
US Special Forces 1945 to the
 Present
The British Army in Northern
 Ireland
Israeli Defence Forces, 1948 to
 the Present
British Special Forces, 1945 to
 Present
US Army Uniforms Europe,
 1944–1945
The French Foreign Legion
Modern American Soldier
Israeli Elite Units
US Airborne Forces of World
 War Two
The Boer War
The Commandos World War
 Two to the Present
Victorian Colonial Wars

A catalogue listing these series and other Arms & Armour Press titles is available on request from: Sales Department, Arms & Armour Press, Artillery House, Artillery Row, London SW1P 1RT.